Potty T

Discover How to Quickly and Easily Potty Train Your Son

By Judith Brooks

Table of Contents

Potty Training Boys – Answers to Your Questions and Tips for Success

Potty training can seem like an overwhelming developmental milestone, both for parents and for their young children. However, if it is broken down into manageable steps it can help both you and your little one transition through the steps of this milestone more easily.

The big question: When to Start Potty Training?

The average age for boys to gain daytime control over their bladder is between the ages of 2 and 3 years of age, but there are also some boys who are ready by 18 months of age and those who aren't until they are 31/2 years or even older. The control and readiness for potty training is rarely present before 18 months of age, especially in boys, because their bodies haven't matured physically enough to make this process successful and they haven't yet grown to be emotionally mature enough to grasp all of the concepts related to potty training. It is also common that nighttime dryness will take more time to achieve, sometimes meaning that boys need to wear diapers or disposable underwear until they are 3 or 4 years of age.

If you're about to begin potty training your son, or perhaps you've started and can't seem to make any progress, review the following tips and guidelines to help you and your little boy through this important milestone. There are readiness signs for which you can look, tips to help the process go more smoothly, pitfalls to avoid, and ideas for achieving nighttime dryness.

Is My Son Ready for Potty Training?
The Signs of Physical Development and When to Start Potty Training

Successful potty training can't easily begin without your son having reached certain physical developmental milestones. His body needs to have matured enough so that the bladder can send a signal to the brain that it is full, and he needs to have enough cognitive maturity to recognize that sign in his brain. Your son's body also needs to have enough muscle control so that he is able to control his bladder once it reaches this point. It is a matter of learning how to coordinate all of these signals and muscles – something that can take time, practice, and patience from both parents and children.

It is not unusual for boys to show these developmental signs at slightly older ages than girls as their maturation ages are slightly older. Sometimes the signs that your son's body has physically developed enough and he is emotionally ready to begin potty training are subtle, but they are important clues you can look for to know that your child is ready for the next steps.

The Skills – Often the skills associated with potty training readiness seem to have little to do with bathroom activities. In order for boys to be ready for the steps it takes for potty training it is important that they have mastered some basic motor skills. If he is climbing, running, creeping through forts, and has reached general motor skill milestones for average 2 to 3 year-olds, his muscle control is starting to be ready for the task of potty training.

The Look – Have you ever seen a look cross your son's face just before he has a wet diaper or bowel movement? That "look" often indicates a realization of what is about to happen with his body. It is often one of the first signs that a child is becoming more aware of his potty habits. Sometimes that look doesn't appear until as your child is in the process of urinating or having a bowel movement, or even after, but watch for the signs such as *the look* that your son is aware of the process in his body.

The Pause – Infants have wet and messy diapers without much, if any, interruption in their current activity. They might wet their diaper while nursing, sleeping, or even just playing with toys and there is no pause in their activity level that indicates the physical change. As boys reach the developmental stage where they are ready to begin potty training, they will likely "pause" what they are doing just before or during urination or having a bowel movement. If you see your son playing, then pause and maybe sit or stand still for several seconds, then resume playing, check to see if he has a wet or messy diaper. These subtle changes in his behavior can indicate a physical awareness that is needed for successful potty training.

The Talk – Potty talk is one of the most important signs for which to look when deciding if your son is ready for potty training. This means that he is able to communicate well enough and shows some verbal interest in leaving the diapers behind. You can encourage this by trying some of the following:

> Teach him the proper names of his body parts. In order to use them well, your son should know what to call each part of his body. This self-awareness is important not only for potty training, but for learning the skills of personal hygiene as well.

> Talk about the diapers. When you change your young son's diapers, tell him that you are changing his diaper

because it is wet or has a poopy diaper. It is wet because there is urination (or pee) in the diaper that came from his body or it is a messy diaper because there is stool in it. Without using any pressure tactics you can also tell him that some day when he is ready he won't need diapers anymore because he will learn to pee and have a bowel movement in the toilet like Daddy does.

Give it some names. Some parents opt for pee and poo, while others prefer more technical terms such as urinate or defecate. No matter which ones you choose, just make sure your child is given some vocabulary to describe this very natural process.

Talk about potty time. Let it be a part of the general conversation that using the bathroom is a normal part of daily life. Children learn by doing and your son can become aware of using the bathroom as a typical part of life when he understands that everyone else in the family uses the bathroom for potty purposes, too.

The Dance – When children begin to be aware of their bodies' needs to use the bathroom they might do the "potty dance" where they fidget and wiggle. Look for this sign that your son either needs to urinate or have a bowel movement. As you begin to recognize your son's potty dance it can be a sign that his body is sending his brain the signals that something needs to happen, even if your son doesn't understand the message quite yet. You can ask him with a gentle reminder such as, "It looks like you're getting a little squirmy – do you think your body is trying to tell you it is potty time?"

The Diaper Ditch – Toddlers often begin to show a negative reaction to wet or messy diapers when they are ready to begin potty training. Young children are often motivated by a need for change, and if your son decides he doesn't like a sagging diaper getting in the way of his tricycle riding, that might be all the motivation he needs to ditch the diapers and start potty training. You can even take his messy diapers and dump the stool into the toilet and let him flush it to reinforce the idea that this is where the stool goes. If he wants to flush it on his own, then make sure to encourage him to wash his hands.

The Schedule – One of the most subtle signs you can look for when determining if your son is ready for potty training is his diaper schedule. Does he stay dry during a nap? Does he awake in the morning without a poopy diaper? Does he have fewer wet diapers during the day? Does he have a bowel movement in the morning? If your son's diaper schedule is becoming more predictable it is good sign that his body is ready for potty training.

The Game of Hide and Seek – Does your son disappear behind the sofa when he has a bowel movement? Seeking a private, quiet moment for potty times is one of the classic signs that your child is aware of his bowels and may be ready for potty training. Often urinating in the toilet is learned before having a bowel movement in the toilet, but the two usually overlap with enough consistency to make this an important sign for which to watch. Your son might also make slight grunting noises or you might see his facial muscles strain.

The Emotions – Yes, even for boys, there is an emotional requirement before they are ready for potty training. Your son needs to be interested in potty training and somewhat care about the results in order for there to be success without battles. He should be able to communicate his feelings with you in some way so that he can let you know if he is frustrated, worried, or looking forward to the process. Your son's emotional maturity will have just as much to do with a positive potty training experience as his physical readiness will.

What Supplies Do I Need for Potty Training My Son?

Choosing the Right Potty Training Tools for Boys

Do I need a potty chair?

The size of your toilet, the location of your bathroom, and the preference of your son to sit or stand while peeing will all influence you decision to use or not use a potty chair. Your son might also simply have a preference for one or the other. Let him use what is most comfortable for him, even if it sometimes requires more clean-up effort on your part.

Whether or not you need a potty chair – or two – depends on many different factors. The first is logistics. If your toilet is tall it might be very difficult for your young son to either climb for sitting on the potty or to stand before it if he prefers to stand as he pees.

Some boys also see potty time as interference in playtime. Using a potty chair in a more convenient location, especially if your bathroom is located on a different floor or area from your living area, can make potty training less of an interruption on his daily playtime routines. A potty chair can also allow your son to "see" his success even if he only pees a very small amount into the reservoir.

If you decide to select a potty chair for your son, look for one with a detachable guard in front. These usually slide on and off and help to prevent urine from splashing out. Young boys don't automatically come equipped with the ability to coordinate their muscles and aim their urine streams. These guards can help minimize the mess while they are learning these skills. A detachable guard will can then be removed as your child becomes more experienced and for cleaning purposes.

Another option is a potty chair seat attachment for your regular toilet. These are mini seats that attach on top of the regular bowl or seat. Using these can help your child have a bowel movement directly into the toilet and eliminate some of the clean-up mess for you. However, if your son is learning to stand while peeing, make sure that your training toilet seat does not get in the way if he needs to quickly use the toilet. By the time you get the seat detached it might be too late.

Should I teach my son to sit or stand?

One of the most common questions parents of boys ask is *how* they should teach their sons to use the bathroom for urination. Peeing while standing for a slightly uncoordinated and easily distracted boy might seem like a huge mess waiting to clean up every time in the bathroom. However, unless medical conditions prevent it, most boys will eventually urinate while standing. This is a necessary skill your son will need to develop in order to use many public restrooms as well. If you're ready to teach your son about standing during urination, try these helpful potty training tips for boys for less mess and more success.

Seeing is believing – Sometimes the best teacher for how this actually works it to allow your son to watch his father use the bathroom. Kids are curious about how things work, and seeing a male parent use the bathroom can help show your son how to use the bathroom while standing.

Aiming – If your son prefers to stand while peeing, give him a target in the toilet to help improve his aim and decrease the mess. Very small, flushable, biodegradable items such as bits of cereal that float are easy and inexpensive methods for improving success. Keep a small plastic bag or container in the bathroom just for this purpose, and when your son is ready to use the bathroom while standing, toss in a small handful of a dozen or so floating targets. This will help to keep your son's eyes on the toilet and improve his hand eye coordination.

Controlling – Urinating while standing takes a bit of practice and control. Teach your son to use one hand to control his penis and aim his urine stream into the toilet. This is another reason why letting your son see his father use the bathroom can help him understand how to do this same thing on his own. Even if your son prefers to sit on the potty, or is sitting on the potty for a bowel movement and then needs to pee, he will often need to use his hand to guide his penis into a position that points the stream downward. Many potty chairs or attachable seats include a splash guard that rises up in front to help eliminate urine from splashing out. If you use one of these guards, be sure to still teach control for times when those guards won't be available.

Should I use diapers while my son is in potty training?

One of the biggest time and money savers for parents when it comes to successful potty training is the ability to stop using diapers and start using underwear, especially during the daytime. Whether or not you continue to use diapers during the potty training experience will depend on a few factors.

Your child's preference – Many children are eager to wear "big boy" underwear as a sign that they are learning to use the bathroom and getting older. If this is your child, consider supporting that preference by switching to one of three options:

1. **Disposable underwear** – These are very similar to diapers, yet can sometimes even cost more, and pull up more like underwear. They can give some kids, especially those who are having limited success, the feeling that they are moving past diapers. Other kids use these during the night to help keep the bed dry during potty training. Some kids, however, don't respond well to disposable underwear because they either feel too much like they are wearing a diaper or because they don't have a sense of wetness that alerts them to their urination. You can find disposable underwear that are specifically designed for boys with more absorbency in the front, where they are more likely to have wetness.
2. **Training pants** – More like underwear but with a thick layer of absorbency, training pants can be a great option for kids who are still prone to accidents but want to wear "big kid" underwear. You can even find training pants with an outer plastic liner that provides an extra layer of protection between clothing and the wetness.

These get washed with your regular laundry, although some with plastic liners need to be line-dried so check the labels first.

3. **Underwear** – As your child consistently shows signs that he is ready for potty training, underwear is sometimes the best option. You should be prepared to do extra loads of laundry during this process, and remember to have extra clothes and underwear available. Take your son shopping and encourage him to choose his own big boy pants. There are different options for him, including boxers, boxer briefs, and regular cut underwear. Some boys like the option of the boxers that allow for easier urination while standing and some kids prefer to get their favorite cartoon characters on their briefs. Just be sure to get enough of whichever style your son chooses so that you can consistently encourage your son to wear the underwear, even on days with many accidents.

Your schedule – If you are consistently on the go with your child, potty training boys can be more challenging and moving right into underwear might mean many extra stops and awkward messes to clean – with fewer resources. Disposable underwear can be the best option for beginners who are away from home (or a regular home base). Some parents prefer to have their children wear underwear around the house and then disposable underwear when they go out to the park, the museum, or to friends' houses. Just be careful to be consistent and make sure your son knows this isn't a message that during these times he doesn't have to use the bathroom.

Your finances – You'll need to weigh the cost differences between regularly buying disposable underwear or buying many pairs of regular underwear, plus a lot of cleaning supplies and extra laundry soap. Sometimes convenience is more valuable for busy parents, but the biggest guiding factor should be how your child reacts to one or the other.

Do I need wet wipes or moist, disposable wipes for my son while he is potty training?

When your son was much younger you probably used some form of wet wipe to clean his bottom when you changed his diaper after he had a bowel movement. You will now have to teach your son how to wipe his own bottom while he is sitting on the potty chair. Especially in the beginning it can be an easier task if he has wet wipes, but you do not have to use them in order to help him learn more about personal hygiene.

Potty Training Boys – How Do I Start?

As mentioned earlier, the first step is to look for those early physical and emotional signs that your son is ready to begin the process of potty training. It is far better to wait until you are confident that he is physically and emotionally ready for this step than to push him, nag him, or create a frustrating situation for both of you. Unless your child faces medical problems, potty training will eventually happen, so be sure to wait for the best opportunity to begin with a cooperative child who is looking forward to this "big boy" step.

- The next step you can take in potty training boys is to make sure that you have all of your supplies – a potty chair, disposable underwear, briefs, wet wipes, and anything else you've chosen to help your child reach this milestone.

- Be enthusiastic with your child as you show him where everything thing is. If you have decided to use a potty chair outside of the bathroom, make sure your son knows where it is and feels comfortable in that location of the home.
- The best time to start is when you can have at least most of the day at home and when you don't have an overwhelmingly busy week scheduled. Start in the morning when your son is well rested and you don't have to rush out the door.
- Schedule potty breaks, even at home, so that you help yourself and your son remember to use the bathroom before it is too late. Several times throughout the day, encourage your child to sit on the potty chair without the disposable diaper on, just to get a sense of how it feels to sit on the potty. If your son wants to stand before the toilet, just remember to have a stool nearby on which he can stand if he needs it for better aim into the toilet without spraying the wall or anything else.
- If your son is fidgety and doesn't want to sit on the toilet you can offer him a book to look at while he sits there to help focus his attention on something else other than just sitting.
- When your child tells you it's time to get off the potty, make sure that he can and that he feels in control of the bathroom situation to a certain extent. You can offer him such phrases as, "You are getting older now and can choose to use the bathroom. You help decide when you need to use it."

- Don't force your son to remain either seated at the potty or standing in front of the stool. This will only build resentment and not help create a positive experience for either one of you. Potty training boys takes time and your son might not get the hang of it for months. Be supportive and positive, and acknowledge when he tries by sitting on the potty chair, even if nothing happens after that.
- Keep watching for those signs that your son either needs to urinate or have a bowel movement. He might wiggle, do the potty dance, grunt, or try to quietly move to the corner of the room. When you see these signs, be sure to help your child get to the bathroom or potty chair as soon as possible.
- If you use a potty chair, have your son help you flush away the waste once he has finished using the bathroom. It will remind him of the whole process, and then you can go with him to wash your hands. Make sure that your son washes his hands after every bathroom visit. Keep a stool near the closest sink so that he can easily access the soap and water. This will help him feel more independent and encourage healthy hygiene habits.
- Let your son know how proud you are of him for taking these steps towards becoming a big boy. Put more emphasis on the effort he puts forth than you do on the accidents he has – and there *will* be accidents.
- Don't punish when there is an accident. Calmly take care of what you need to do with cleaning supplies, but have your son clean himself, either with wet wipes, a warm washcloth, or even by a short shower if needed.

This helps him to understand the importance of hygiene and independence when it comes to bathroom habits.

More Tips Potty Training Tips for Boys

Even the best of preparations can sometimes end with young children who just don't either seem interested or capable of getting on the potty training bandwagon. If you are feeling frustrated and not sure what to do next to help your son learn how to use the bathroom more independently, try some of these tips.

Motivation Charts and Other Incentives

Sometimes there just simply isn't enough intrinsic motivation for your son to want to use the potty just for the sake of learning to be a big boy and take those steps. If your son is losing his enthusiasm but he still is showing the physical and emotional signs of readiness for potty training, consider a motivation chart.

- Take a plain calendar or print a blank calendar for the week or month and hang it at a height where your son can easily see the days.
- Have a basket of small stickers nearby. You can have him earn one sticker for peeing in the potty, two for having a bowel movement in the potty, and a bonus one for keeping himself clean. You can also decide if you want to use a certain sticker amount if your son is learning to stand while peeing and you want him to earn stickers for aiming well.

- For some children the motivation is just in building a collage of stickers on the calendar and that is the only reward that they need.
- For other children, small incentives for earning so many stickers can help increase potty training success. Some simple reward ideas for a predetermined number of earned stickers can include:
    o Trips to his favorite park
    o An extra bedtime story
    o A favorite afternoon snack in the backyard
    o A new book
    o A small toy – don't go overboard on the monetary investment or the stakes will only get higher
    o A homemade coupon to choose what is served for dinner, play a game with Dad after he comes home from work, or help from Mom cleaning up the toys on the living room floor
    o Choosing a new pair of underwear with his favorite characters printed on them
- Don't remove stickers for accidents. It will turn the motivation chart into a scorecard instead and the positive reinforcement will be gone.
- Use verbal praise when he gets to add stickers to the chart, too. Your enthusiasm will help to keep him excited about his growing independence.
- If you are worried that your child will be using the bathroom only to earn the stickers, it won't be the worst problem you encounter. Your child will only be able to physically, actually use the bathroom so many times. Either way, the motivation is working and your son is learning to use the bathroom as needed (even if

he goes a few extra times just to earn some more stickers).

Outside Potties

To pee outside or not – that is the question. Something about nature calling seems to call to boys to urinate outside so as to not interrupt their playtime and to have a better chance at making it to the bathroom on time. If you live in a rural area, especially if you end up far away from the house, it can be easier to allow your child to use the bathroom outside than to try to make a mad dash to the house to use the bathroom (only to end up needing to clean up and change clothes). It is a personal family decision whether or not you'll let your son use the bathroom outdoors when needed. Just be sure that he is still practicing good hygiene and that he clearly understands the difference between using the tree in the woods for his potty target and using the fire hydrant at his friend's house in town.

Public Restrooms

Your little boy might be feeling some large-sized independence as he learns to use the potty. When it comes time for him to use the public restroom there are some extra things you'll want to consider and talk about with your son before the time strikes. If you're the mom it isn't practical that you'll be able to scope out the public men's restroom before your son uses it to make sure there is toilet paper, paper towels he can reach, and a safe environment overall. Until he is really old enough to manage independently and safely on his own, look for either a family restroom or explain to him ahead of time that when he needs to use the restroom while shopping, at the museum, or other places, that he needs to go with Mom if Dad or an older brother isn't available.

Dress for Success

Even if your son's favorite outfit is his pair of blue overalls, potty training is not the time to worry about snaps, hooks, and even zippers. Make sure you have some weather appropriate clothes with elastic waistbands that your son can easily pull on and off by himself.

The other option is to allow him to go bare-bottom in the house while he explores his newfound diaper-less freedom. If you decide to allow him to go without bottoms for a few days while he learns to spend more time on the potty chair, don't be surprised if you see him touching his genitals. This is a new experience for your son and personal exploration is a natural part of that process. Don't admonish him for doing so because you don't want him to get the message that his private body parts are bad things, but just make sure that he is practicing proper hygiene with frequent hand washing.

Potty Training on the Go

Families are busy and it can be very challenging to attempt potty training when it seems like you aren't home for more than a few hours at a time each day. A busy schedule, however, doesn't have to mean that you have to delay potty training.

Get all of your son's caregivers on board with your potty training plan and make sure that everyone approaches it in the same way. For example, if you are encouraging your son to stand while urinating, make sure everyone else is aware of that so they don't try to insist that he sit on the toilet.

Make a portable motivation chart if you're using one. You can add it into your planner or even find a free and easy to use app for tracking potty breaks on the go with your son. Another option is to purchase an inexpensive pocket calendar that you can toss in your son's backpack with an envelope or baggie filled with the small stickers. Just make sure that whatever motivation chart you're using is easily accessible so there is an immediate reward factor possible.

Pack several sets of extra clothes, underwear, disposable underwear, and wet wipes. You can even just leave this extra bag in your vehicle during the potty training process. Don't forget to add in a few empty plastic shopping bags to use to store any wet or messy clothes from accidents.

If your child spends time at a daycare or another family member's home, have two sets of all of the basic supplies there. This includes an extra potty chair or toilet seat like the one you are using at your home, extra clothes, underwear, training pants, and disposable underwear, as well as wet wipes and a motivation chart.

Make a plan for potty stops along the way. There are even apps available that can help you pinpoint public restrooms while you are travelling. Just make sure that you schedule in several potty breaks so that your child has every opportunity to use a bathroom. When kids are busy shopping, playing with friends, or running other errands with you they can become easily distracted and forget to listen to those signals from their bodies. Help remind your son by occasionally asking him if he needs to use the potty. Even if he says no, take him on a regular schedule, especially during the beginning of potty training, so that he doesn't have to go too long without a bathroom immediately available.

A busy lifestyle doesn't mean that you won't be able to potty train your son. It might take some more planning, a bit more patience, and an extra bag of supplies, but it can be done. The key is to be consistent both at home and away with expectations, and encourage your son every step of the way.

Potty Training Regression and Pitfalls

There are a few pitfalls that parents and caregivers should avoid during potty training. Even though potty training boys can seem like it takes a long time and much energy, giving in to these pitfalls only makes the experience more difficult for everyone.

Punishing

There will be accidents during potty training – it is natural for your son to make mistakes as he learns to listen to the signals his body is sending. Punishment for accidents and messes only adds negativity to the situation. If you feel yourself getting more and more frustrated with the number of accidents your son is having, take an inventory of several factors by asking yourself some questions:

- Is my son *really* ready for potty training or did we start before he showed many of those important signs of readiness?
- Am I providing him with all of the tools necessary for him to be successful? (i.e. potty chair, wet wipes for easier cleaning, motivation chart)
- Am I praising him for his successes?
- How can I keep myself calm when he has multiple accidents each day? (i.e. slowing down the schedule so you have more time during the day, breathing deeply and counting to 25 before cleaning up the mess)

Fluid Restriction

It can be tempting to do things like reduce the amount of fluid that your son drinks in order to reduce the number of accidents he has while potty training, but this is not a healthy or helpful idea. Your son won't be able to learn to use the bathroom on a consistent schedule if you interrupt his typical liquid consumption. Plus, there are health risks to restricting fluids in children who can't always monitor for themselves how thirsty and dehydrated they feel. In fact, if you are going to be at home for a few days and can really concentrate on potty training, encourage your son to keep a water bottle with him for whenever he is thirsty. The more natural opportunities he has to use the bathroom, the more opportunities he has to learn to listen to his body signals that it is time to go.

Boomerang Potty Training

Do you encourage your son to wear underwear one day, and then hand him disposable underwear the next? Boomerang potty training refers to an inconsistent approach that usually results from two things: accidents that make parents second-guess their son's readiness and a change in routine that makes it less convenient to potty train. Either one of these reasons can end in the same result – a boy who is confused about potty training.

Once you have made an assessment that your son is ready for potty training because he has been showing those necessary physical and emotional signals and you have started down that path to diaper free days – stay on that path. Consistency in your approach and your dedication will signal to your son that this is an important milestone and that you are supporting him – no matter how many accidents he has or how busy your life gets.

Bumps Along the Way

There are bound to be bumps along the way to diaper free days. If your child becomes ill during the potty training process it can make things much more challenging. Things such as fevers and diarrhea make it much more difficult to predict your child's bathroom habits and your son will likely find it much more difficult to succeed. If your son does become ill, talk with him about how sometimes when our bodies are sick it can make it much harder to learn things, so it is OK to use things like disposable underwear during these times. You can still encourage him to use the bathroom when he is feeling able, but this way you haven't totally reversed the potty training and you're allowing him to recover from his illness without the stress of potty training.

Emotional stresses can also cause your child to have more accidents or potty training regression. Sometimes this is a sign that your son is stressed about an event or situation. Have patience with him and help him find ways to deal with the stress

– you can spend more time playing together, having quiet reading time, or slowing down a hectic pace.

When Do I Start Nighttime Potty Training For My Son?

Nighttime potty training usually happens after your son has reached two other important milestones: daytime potty success with minimal accidents and dry diapers or disposable underwear in the morning. Nighttime dryness can take months longer to achieve, especially for boys. In order to make the transition into diaper free nights, follow some of these basic principles and tips.

> Use a plastic mattress cover. While you are helping your son learn to stay dry at night there are bound to be accidents. A plastic mattress cover will help to protect the mattress and reduce the time and effort you have to spend cleaning, especially during the middle of the night.

> Have extra fitted sheets on hand. If your son wakes up in the middle of the night and is wet the last thing you'll want to have to do is search for another sheet.

> Consider using disposable underwear, especially at first. It might take some time for your son to get into the habit of waking to use the bathroom if needed and disposable underwear can help him to feel like he is working toward that goal but keep him comfortable while in his bed.

Reduce the amount of liquid he has access to in the hours before bedtime. You don't need to have a total restriction, but it will be more challenging for him to stay dry at night if he just drinks two glasses of apple juice before he brushes his teeth before bed.

Keep a nightlight on in the bathroom or in the hallway near the bathroom so your son can find his way. This is the first time he will be learning to navigate his way during the night so you'll want to make sure he has easy and safe access to the bathroom when he needs it.

Take the time to wake your son up at least once during the night and lead him into the bathroom. You can do this just before you go to bed if he has been sleeping for a few hours, or you can set your alarm to wake later – just don't wait too long or it may be too late. By waking your son and leading him to the bathroom you are helping him train his brain to wake from sleep and use the bathroom.

One of the benefits of teaching your son to urinate while standing is that nighttime potty trips can be much easier if all he has to do is walk into the bathroom and stand before the toilet. Make sure his pajamas are easy to pull down and up and his pajama shirt isn't too long. Long pajama shirts can get in the way of his urination stream, and when he is sleepy the last thing you want to have to worry about is a successful trip to the bathroom where you still have to change him because his pajamas got in the way.

Just as with daytime dryness, nighttime potty training success can be interrupted by illness, stress, or changes in your child's routine. It is important to have patience and be as consistent as possible. If your son does wear underwear or training pants to bed and wakes up wet, help him quietly and quickly get cleaned and changed so that he can still get a good night's rest. Sometimes having a sleeping bag handy is easier than making the bed again, especially if it is getting close to morning and the chances of another accident are lower. Just strip the sheets off the bed, wipe down the mattress cover with a damp cloth with mild cleaner, wipe dry, and then place the sleeping bag on top of the mattress cover.

Nighttime dryness does not come as easily for every boy. In fact, boys are more likely than girls to experience bedwetting issues as they get older. These can come and go or bedwetting can persist into the late elementary years. Genetics appear to play a role in whether or not your son may experience bedwetting as he gets older. If nighttime dryness just doesn't seem possible for your son on a consistent basis, and he was never really able to remain dry night after night, consult with his pediatrician. It is likely something that he will just have to outgrow and for which both you and your son will need patience. There are limited use medications available that act in essence in reverse of diuretics, preventing the kidneys from producing urine during the night. These can be used on very limited basis, under the guidance of a physician, for things such as sleep-away camps or slumber parties with friends.

However, if your son was successful at achieving nighttime dryness and didn't need to wear disposable underwear while sleeping for extended periods of time and then starts experiencing bedwetting, this can be a sign of a problem. Sometimes emotional issues result in bedwetting and other times physical illnesses can be to blame. An occasion night of bedwetting may just be a result of a really deep sleep on those nights, and not necessarily a result of potty training regression. However, if your son begins bedwetting for no apparent reason, consult with his pediatrician to see if there is an underlying cause or condition.

Potty Training Boys – Conclusion

Potty training is one of those milestones that seems to loom so large when you first begin down that path with your son. However, with the right tools, a dose of enthusiasm, and two doses of patience, you can help your son be diaper free. If at any time during the training process your son complains of pain during urination or when having a bowel movement consult with his pediatrician. It may be the sign of a urinary tract infection or something such as constipation.